Rural Life, Urban Life

Caryl McDonald

INFOMAX COMMON CORE READERS

Rosen Classroom™

New York

Published in 2014 by The Rosen Publishing Group, Inc.
29 East 21st Street, New York, NY 10010

Book Design: Michael J. Flynn

Photo Credits: Cover, p. 5 Vasaleks/Shutterstock.com; p. 7 Kimberly Hall/Shutterstock.com; p. 9 ValeStock/Shutterstock.com; p. 11 Orientaly/Shutterstock.com; p. 13 Songquan Deng/Shutterstock.com; p. 15 Bruce MacQueen/Shutterstock.com; p. 17 Jorg Hackemann/Shutterstock.com; p. 19 ASchindl/Shutterstock.com; p. 21 (top) Jonathan G/Shutterstock.com; p. 21 (bottom) Richard Cavalleri/Shutterstock.com.

ISBN: 978-1-4777-2346-3
6-pack ISBN: 978-1-4777-2347-0

Manufactured in the United States of America

CPSIA Compliance Information: Batch #CS13RC: For further information contact Rosen Publishing, New York, New York at 1-800-237-9932.

Contents

The Big City

James lives in a big city with his family. His family's house is in an urban area. Urban places are big cities. There's always a lot to do there. James likes living in a city, but he likes visiting other places, too.

There are a lot of neat places to explore in an urban area.

Going to Grandma's

One of James's favorite places to go is his grandma's house. James has to drive a long way to get there. It's really far from the city. That's because James's grandma lives in a rural area. Rural places are in the country. Rural life is very different from urban life!

How do you think living in the country is different from living in the city?

Noisy and Quiet

James's neighborhood has a lot of tall buildings. There are many places nearby to visit, like **restaurants** and other businesses. There are always loud cars and buses driving around. Most of all, there are a lot of people. The busy **activity** in James's city makes it a noisy place to live!

The people and cars in a city can make a lot of noise.

1570

There are only a few buildings near James's grandma's house. They're shorter than the buildings in the city. There aren't as many people, so there are fewer restaurants and stores. When James goes to his grandma's house, he thinks it seems very quiet.

Country life is known for being quiet and relaxing.

City Plants, Country Plants

James's city has more buildings than grass and other plants. James's house is **surrounded** by sidewalks, streets, and buildings. Some buildings have plants near them, but not all of them do. James likes to go to the city's beautiful parks. That's where he usually sees plants and animals.

People in the city like to keep plants around so they can be around nature, too.

The country is full of pretty plants and wild animals. James's grandma has a big lawn with tall trees and colorful flowers. She also has woods behind her house. Deer, rabbits, and other animals live quietly in the woods. James likes to see them run quickly through the trees!

Many different kinds of animals live in the woods. If you're not quiet, you may scare them away!

Different Kinds of Fun

James does a lot of fun things in the city. He goes with his family to **museums**. They see old paintings and learn about history. James likes to go shopping at all the different stores. In the city, a lot of fun things take place indoors.

Cities are great places for learning about history and how our world used to be.

When James visits his grandma, he spends a lot of time outdoors. He camps with his cousins during the summer. They swim in the lake and climb trees. In the winter, the country gets a lot of snow. He can do fun things, like make snowmen and snow angels.

Living in the country lets you do many fun outdoor activities.

Going Home

James likes visiting his grandma, but he likes going home, too. He knows he'll see his grandma again soon. Visiting her shows James how urban and rural areas are different. Is your neighborhood rural or urban? What do you like about living there?

Which one do you like better, the city or the country?

urban

rural

Urban Life and Rural Life

urban	rural
buildings	nature everywhere
sidewalks	fewer people
many stores	outdoor activities
museums	open space
nature in parks	lots of wild animals

Glossary

activity (ak-TIH-vuh-tee) Everything that people around you are doing.

museum (myoo-ZEE-uhm) A place for keeping and showing art or objects from long ago.

restaurant (REHS-tuh-rahnt) A place to buy and eat a meal.

surround (suh-ROUND) To shut something in on all sides.

Index